DATE DUE

MAY 3 0			
MAY 3 0			

DEMCO 38-296

Childhoods
of the
Presidents

George Washington

Childhoods *of the* Presidents

John Adams

George W. Bush

Bill Clinton

Ulysses S. Grant

Andrew Jackson

Thomas Jefferson

John F. Kennedy

Abraham Lincoln

James Madison

James Monroe

Ronald Reagan

Franklin D. Roosevelt

Theodore Roosevelt

Harry S. Truman

George Washington

Woodrow Wilson

George
Washington

Gail Snyder

Mason Crest Publishers
Philadelphia

Produced by OTTN Publishing, Stockton, New Jersey

Mason Crest Publishers
370 Reed Road
Broomall, PA 19008
www.masoncrest.com

First printing

1 3 5 7 9 8 6 4 2

Library of Congress Cataloging-in-Publication Data

Snyder, Gail.
    George Washington / Gail Snyder.
        p.   cm.   (Childhood of the presidents)
    Summary: A biography of the first president of the United
    States, focusing on his childhood and young adulthood.
    Includes bibliographical references (p.) and index.
        ISBN 1-59084-270-7
    1. Washington, George, 1732-1799—Childhood and youth—
    Juvenile literature. 2. Washington, George, 1732-1799—Juvenile
    literature. 3. Presidents—United States—Biography—Juvenile
    literature. [1. Washington, George, 1732-1799—Childhood and
    youth. 2. Presidents.] I. Title. II. Series.
    E312.66.S69 2003
    973.4'1'092—dc21
    [B]   2002069245

Childhoods
of the
Presidents

Table of Contents

★★★★★★★★★★★★★★★★★★

Introduction...6
Arthur M. Schlesinger, jr.

Leaving Home 9

Young Man with a Temper 15

Minding His Manners 21

The Secret Plan 25

Reluctant President 33

Chronology 42

Glossary 43

Further Reading 44

Internet Resources 45

Index 46

★*Introduction*★

Alexis de Tocqueville began his great work *Democracy in America* with a discourse on childhood. If we are to understand the prejudices, the habits and the passions that will rule a man's life, Tocqueville said, we must watch the baby in his mother's arms; we must see the first images that the world casts upon the mirror of his mind; we must hear the first words that awaken his sleeping powers of thought. "The entire man," he wrote, "is, so to speak, to be seen in the cradle of the child."

That is why these books on the childhoods of the American presidents are so much to the point. And, as our history shows, a great variety of childhoods can lead to the White House. The record confirms the ancient adage that every American boy, no matter how unpromising his beginnings, can aspire to the presidency. Soon, one hopes, the adage will be extended to include every American girl.

All our presidents thus far have been white males who, within the limits of their gender, reflect the diversity of American life. They were born in nineteen of our states; eight of the last thirteen presidents were born west of the Mississippi. Of all our presidents, Abraham Lincoln had the least promising childhood, yet he became our greatest president. Oddly enough, presidents who are children of privilege sometimes feel an obligation to reform society in order to give children of poverty a better break. And, with Lincoln the great exception, presidents who are children of poverty sometimes feel that there is no need to reform a society that has enabled them to rise from privation to the summit.

Does schooling make a difference? Harry S. Truman, the only twentieth-century president never to attend college, is generally accounted a near-great president. Actually nine— more than one fifth—of our presidents never went to college at all, including such luminaries as George Washington, Andrew Jackson and Grover Cleveland. But, Truman aside, all the non-college men held the highest office before the twentieth century, and, given the increasing complexity of life, a college education will unquestionably be a necessity in the twenty-first century.

Every reader of this book, girls included, has a right to aspire to the presidency. As you survey the childhoods of those who made it, try to figure out the qualities that brought them to the White House. I would suggest that among those qualities are ambition, determination, discipline, education— and luck.

—ARTHUR M. SCHLESINGER, JR.

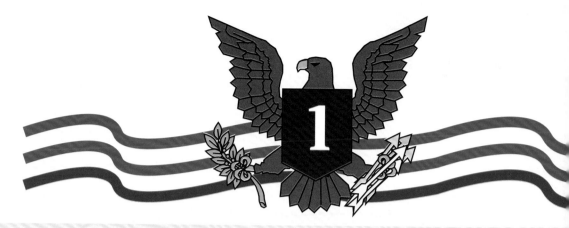

This painting shows George Washington and his partner, Christopher Gist, poling a raft across the Allegheny River during a surveying expedition. George got his first surveying experience at the age of 16.

Leaving Home

*I*n the spring of 1748, Thomas Fairfax decided to find out exactly what the king of England had given him. Lord Fairfax, a wealthy colonist in Virginia, had been granted five million acres of land west of the Blue Ridge Mountains in the Shenandoah Valley. Five million acres is an enormous area—about the size of the entire state of New Jersey. Fairfax's piece of land was so large, in fact, that he could not personally visit it all himself. He needed help determining what the land was like, what it could be used for, and whether people were living on it without his permission. To find out, he hired a *surveyor* named James Genn, who would use special instruments to chart Fairfax's holdings and divide them into lots that could be sold to other people.

Fairfax also invited a young neighbor of his to join the surveying party. Though just 16, George Washington looked like a man. At six feet two inches tall, with long legs and large hands, George was bigger than most men. Yet the redheaded youth had never before taken a trip without his family.

The trip "over the mountain" lasted a little more than a month, but that was long enough to change George's life. It gave him a chance to try out his own skills as a surveyor, which he had begun to build when he was 15 and discovered surveying instruments once owned by his father.

Surveyors relied on two tools to do their jobs: a compass, for determining direction; and a 33-foot iron chain with 50 links, to measure distance. This heavy chain had to be handled by two people, the lead chainman and the rear chainman. These two had the difficult task of maneuvering the chain around trees, brush, and other objects that got in the way of measuring a straight line.

After the surveyor determined the starting mark, the lead chainman walked to that spot. Then the rear chainman stretched out the chain, bringing one end to the spot where the lead chainman was standing. Next, the lead chainman used an iron pin to mark the spot where the chain ended. The rear chainman then moved forward with the chain, dangling the end of it where the pin had been set. The two men would continue stretching out the chain and setting pins until all 10 they carried had been used. They could then tell that they had measured five chains. Eighty chains equaled one mile.

George was a surveyor's assistant on the trip over the Blue Ridge Mountains. He took care of the horses, cleared the underbrush, and helped the chainmen carry the equipment.

For all that physical work George was paid a Spanish doubloon—the equivalent of seven dollars—a day. In America at that time there was no official currency, so many foreign coins were used.

More important than the pay, though, was the fact that George got his first opportunity to see what life was like on the

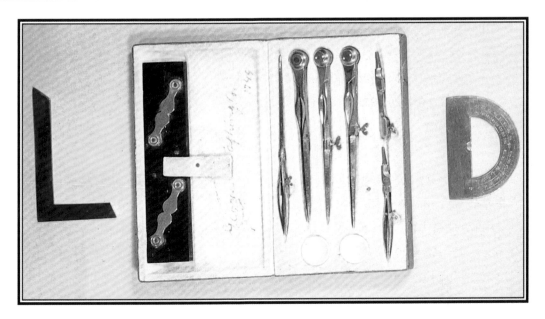

These 18th-century drafting instruments belonged to George Washington, whose signature can be seen on the box. The tools would have been used to create maps of surveyed land.

frontier, where the comforts of home were lacking. A record of George's trip still exists in the first diary he ever wrote. Keeping a diary was to become a regular activity for him.

In his diary, George writes as someone used to such fine things as a clean four-post bed and dining room tables set with tablecloths and knives. He quickly learned that sleeping out-doors in front of a fire had advantages over sleeping indoors when he was shown to the worst bed he had ever seen at one home in which the surveying party stayed.

"We got our Suppers & was lighted into a Room & I not being so good a Woodsman as the rest of my Company," he wrote, "stripped myself very orderly & went into the Bed as they called it when to my Surprize I found it to be nothing but a Little Straw-Matted together without Sheets or any thing

Within a year of the Fairfax expedition, George Washington had passed a test at the College of William and Mary (shown here) to become a certified surveyor.

else, but only one thread Bear blanket with double its Weight of Vermin such as Lice Fleas etc. I was glad to get up (as soon as the Light was carried from us) & put on my Cloths & Lay as my Companions. Had we not been very tired I am sure we should not have slep'd much that night." (The original spelling, capitalization, and punctuation of the diary is maintained throughout this book.)

Yet sleeping outdoors had its own set of dangers. One evening the wind blew away the men's tent and they spent the night without shelter. Another time the straw on which they were sleeping was ignited by a campfire spark. Luckily the flames were put out before anyone was hurt.

George also had one of his earliest brushes with Native Americans when the surveying party suddenly encountered 30 members of a local tribe. One of the Indians was carrying a scalp, the hair and skin taken from a white man they had killed. Rather than being afraid of them, the teenager and his companion, a cousin of Lord Fairfax, instinctively tried to be friendly. They found some liquor and offered it to the Indians. After drinking the liquor, the warriors began to dance.

In his diary, George described what he saw next: "They clear a Large Circle make a Great Fire in the Middle then seats themselves around it the Speaker makes a grand speech telling them in what Manner they are to Daunce. [A]fter he has finished the best Dauncer Jumps up as one awaked out of a Sleep and Jumps about the Ring in a most comical Manner he is followed by the Rest."

Plagued by nearly constant rain and with supplies running out, George decided to go home after slightly more than a month had gone by. He and Lord Fairfax's cousin mounted their horses and rode off on their own—only to discover that they didn't know where they were going. They rode 20 miles in the wrong direction before they realized their mistake.

George's first experience as a paid surveyor's assistant was a good one, though. By the time he was 17, after he had passed a test at William and Mary College in Williamsburg, Virginia, he was a certified surveyor. He quickly found a job as official surveyor of Culpeper County. George was on his way to his first of many careers: soldier, planter, *legislator*, general, and, finally, president of the United States.

PUBLISHED BY CURRIER & IVES

152 NASSAU ST NEW YORK

THE BIRTH-PLACE OF WASHINGTON.
At Bridges Creek, Westmoreland Co. Va. (Feby. 22nd 1732.)

A 19th-century engraving of the four-room house in Westmoreland County, Virginia, where George Washington was born.

Young Man with a Temper

By the time George was born in 1732, his family had been living in America for 75 years. George's great-grandfathers, John Washington and William Ball, both arrived in Virginia in 1657. In England, both families had supported King Charles I during the English civil war of the 1640s. Also called the Puritan Revolution, the war pitted forces loyal to the king against forces loyal to Parliament and began after Charles attempted to impose the Anglican religion on Presbyterian Scotland. People who sided with the king were called Royalists. When King Charles was defeated, his supporters paid the price for being on the losing side. As their fortunes declined at home, many of them left for the New World. The colony of Virginia became known as a *sanctuary* for Royalists.

At first, John Washington had no intentions of settling in Virginia. A sailor, he planned to pick up tobacco in Virginia and bring it back to England to be sold. But his ship, *Seahorse of London*, sank during a storm. His tobacco was ruined, and he had no way of getting home. He made the best of things.

In America, John Washington restored his family to its former prominence. He served as a *burgess, vestryman, coroner,* president of the county court, and military officer.

Life in the colonies was hard. Many people died young of diseases such as *tuberculosis*, smallpox, and malaria. Many babies did not survive their first year of life. John Washington's son Lawrence died of disease just after starting his own family. His son, Augustine, who was called Gus, was three years old when his father died. He was still a child when his mother passed away as well.

Despite the high death rate, Virginia was an attractive place to settle. Wild turkeys, deer, geese, and other game were plentiful for hunting. Men hoping to become wealthy saved their money to acquire land that could be used to raise tobacco, corn, and livestock. Tobacco was used like money to trade with England for products that could not be purchased in the American colonies.

Gus Washington became a well-to-do man. He operated several large *plantations*, growing tobacco with slave labor. Gus also operated an iron mine. His idea was to supply the British with the iron ore that England formerly bought from Sweden before the countries became enemies.

Gus and his first wife had three children. They were Lawrence, Augustine Jr., and Jane. When his first wife died, Gus quickly remarried, choosing Mary Ball to be his second wife in 1731. At 23, she was 15 years younger than her husband. Like him, Mary had been orphaned as a child. She was tall, agile, and fond of horses.

Eleven months after their wedding, their first child was born, at 10 o'clock in the morning on February 22 in the family's four-room house in Westmoreland County, Virginia. Gus

The story of George Washington admitting to having chopped down his father's cherry tree has become part of American lore, but it is entirely made up. This painting by the American artist Grant Wood shows Parson Mason Weems, who included the story in his 19th-century biography of Washington, drawing back a curtain to show Gus Washington asking his son about the damaged tree.

and Mary Washington named him George after Colonel George Eskridge, Mary's stepfather.

Mary was so delighted with her new baby that she spent a month showing him off to her friends and relatives. It was the only time in his life that she doted on the boy. The special attention ended when she gave birth to more babies in short order. There was Betty, who was a year younger than George; Samuel, two years younger; Jack, four years younger; and Charles, five years younger. Baby Mildred arrived seven years

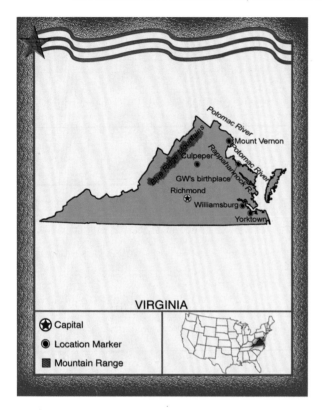

This map of Virginia shows many of the places that figured prominently in George Washington's life.

after George but did not live to see her second birthday. George's half-sister Jane died at 13.

George grew up in a busy household full of children, horses, cows, and pigs. Ten slaves worked at his house, and one of them was charged with watching over him.

George was a shy child, a bit awkward but very likable. He did not spend much time with his father, who was frequently away tending to his various properties and iron mine.

By the time George was seven, his family had moved three times. George's favorite home was Epsewasson, which he called his "home house." Located near the Potomac River, it would later be named Mount Vernon. After his presidency ended, George would retire there.

Gus taught his son how to ride a horse as soon as he was old enough to sit in the saddle, and George became an expert horseman. Later, President Thomas Jefferson described Washington as "the greatest horseman of his age." George learned to hunt, fish, play cards, and dance. His mastery of the hatchet gave him strong arms and may have led to a legend.

Parson Mason Weems, who wrote the first biography of George Washington after his death, made up the well-known story of George refusing to lie after chopping down his father's favorite cherry tree. Intent on making George's life seem perfect and inspirational, Weems also concocted the story of George throwing a silver dollar across the Potomac River.

Far from being the perfect son sometimes depicted, George was a boy with a quick temper who insisted on getting his own way. As an adult, his temper flashed in battle, in meetings with his advisers, and when dealing with Congress. Those who displeased him knew about their offense. But once his temper flared, he usually didn't stay angry long.

His mother was very strict and didn't encourage her children to take risks. One of George's cousins once said about Mary, "I was ten times more afraid [of her] than I ever was of my own parents." Like her son, she was very willful. Some said that she got along better with horses than with people. One of her favorite horses was a bay (reddish brown) *mare* left to her by her stepbrother. George knew that his mother had forbidden him to ride the bay. One day he decided to break the rule. As he leaped on the horse's back, the bay reared and tore a blood vessel in its neck. Mary's favorite horse—healthy a minute before—lay dead. George's mother was furious.

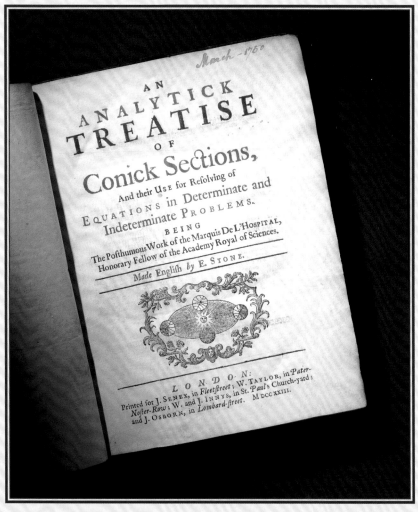

This work on mathematics is believed to be the first book George Washington ever owned. It may have helped him compute the area of irregularly shaped pieces of land. He dated the title page March 1750 at the top.

Minding His Manners

The Washington family had a tradition of sending their sons to boarding school in England. George's much older half-brothers, Lawrence and Augustine, attended the Appleby School, where their father had gone. Gus planned to send George there when he was old enough, too. But he never got the chance.

George was only 11 years old when Gus died suddenly. Mary Washington decided not to send her son to Appleby. Tutors hired by his family and teachers at the country schools he attended provided his education. His formal education ended at about age 14.

Like other pupils, George had to make his own ink and goose quills for writing. He also had to make his own copybooks. George was a very good student, and math was one of his best subjects. *Geometry* and *trigonometry*, subjects that many modern-day students struggle with, were easy for him and would help him later when he became a surveyor.

In George's time, books were expensive and difficult to find. Sometimes students were asked to copy material found in a book into their own copybook, which they could keep.

Mary Ball Washington, George's mother, was strong-willed and strict. She did not send George to the Appleby School, where his father and older brothers had gone, because she was concerned about the family's finances and afraid to have George living away from home.

As an adult, George would become known for his courteous, respectful, and gentlemanly treatment of other people. He began to develop this sensitivity as a child based on the 110 rules of respect first composed by French *Jesuits* in 1595. Later the rules were translated into English in a book called *Rules of Civility and Decent Behavior in Company and Conversation*.

One of George's teachers had him copy the rules into his copybook in his large, clear handwriting. George's ideas about how people should act in a polite society would come into play when he had to decide how he should be addressed as the nation's first president, and in the humbleness he demonstrated when his country called upon him to serve.

Some of the rules may seem funny today, like No. 100: "Cleanse not your teeth with the table cloth napkin, fork or knife; but if others do it, let it be done without a peep to them."

Yet George took them all quite seriously as they reflected situations people were likely to encounter in the 18th century.

At least one of the rules must have spoken directly to George because it discussed holding one's temper. Rule No. 105 said: "Be not angry at table whatever happens and if you have reason to be so, show it not . . . especially if there be strangers."

Another rule that he lived by was No. 32: "To one that is your equal, or not much inferior, you are to give the chief place in your lodging, and he to whom it is offered ought at the first to refuse it, but at the second to accept though not without acknowledging his own unworthiness."

George took the last lesson of humility to heart. When he was named commander of the colonial forces that would fight the American Revolution against England, he told Congress, "I beg it may be remembered that I, this day, declare with the utmost sincerity, I do not think myself equal to the command I am honored with."

Ashamed of his limited education, George did not like to discuss his schooling when he grew older. Of all the presidents, only Andrew Jackson had as little education as George Washington. Yet he had nothing to be ashamed of. He was 22 when he became commander of Virginia's armed forces. Later he would more than hold his own with men like Thomas Jefferson, John Adams, and 24 of the delegates to the Constitutional Convention, all of whom went to college.

Mount Vernon is the second most visited home in America. The first is the White House, which was completed a year after Washington died.

George Washington informs his mother of his plan to go to sea in this rather sentimental engraving. Mary Washington would eventually say no to the idea.

The Secret Plan

*T*hough he died suddenly, Gus Washington had drawn up a will that left his properties to his family. In all there were 10,000 acres of land in seven tracts to be distributed among his sons. His oldest child, Lawrence, got George's favorite home, Epsewasson, which he renamed Mount Vernon. Lawrence had served under General Vernon in bloody fighting at Cartagena, a fortress in Colombia, South America. George was seven years old when England declared war on Spain over an incident at sea. Virginia sent 400 soldiers to assist England in the fighting, which pitted 12,000 Englishmen against 4,000 Spaniards. Despite outnumbering the Spaniards three to one, 9,000 British and colonial soldiers died. As one of four captains to serve under General Vernon, Lawrence was praised for his poise in battle.

While Lawrence got Mount Vernon, 11-year-old George received Ferry Farm, which included 224 acres of land and 10 slaves. He also received 2,291 acres from another tract and three lots in Fredericksburg, Virginia. George's inheritance was to remain under his mother's control until he reached adulthood.

Mount Vernon, George's favorite family home, passed to his older half-brother Lawrence upon the death of their father. As a teen, George spent a great deal of time there with Lawrence and his wife, Anne Fairfax Washington.

After his father's death, George spent many of his summers with his brother Lawrence at Mount Vernon. Lawrence was 14 years older than George, and the younger boy admired him greatly. He remembered how handsome Lawrence looked in his scarlet naval uniform and was proud that Lawrence was considered a war hero.

Shortly after Gus's death, Lawrence married Anne Fairfax. Anne's father, Colonel Fairfax, was the cousin of Lord Fairfax, and his family lived only two miles away from Mount Vernon on their plantation, called Belvoir.

Like the Washingtons and the Balls, the Fairfax family had

supported King Charles in the English civil war. In 1660 the dead king's exiled son, Charles II, was returned to the English throne. King Charles II rewarded the Fairfax family for their loyalty by giving them 5.2 million acres of land in what is now northern Virginia and West Virginia.

Lawrence's marriage into the Fairfax family helped the entire Washington family. Lawrence was elected to the House of Burgesses and George got to spend a lot of time at Belvoir. It didn't take long for George to impress Anne's father, Colonel William Fairfax, with his charm, maturity, and intelligence.

Lawrence worried about how his little brother would make his way in the world. He knew that Ferry Farm would not be enough to support George. He decided that George's best option for a good life would be to go to sea as a member of the

King Charles II (shown here) rewarded the Fairfax family's loyalty to the British crown with an enormous land grant in America. The Fairfaxes, in turn, would play a significant role in the life of young George Washington.

George Washington was one of eight presidents who were born in Virginia. The others were Thomas Jefferson, James Madison, James Monroe, William Henry Harrison, John Tyler, Zachary Taylor, and Woodrow Wilson.

Royal Navy. The Fairfaxes agreed that a life at sea would be a wise choice for the 14-year-old boy. They used their influence to get George a commission as a midshipman in the British navy.

A well-intentioned secret conspiracy was formed. The plotters knew that Mary Washington would not be pleased at the idea of her oldest child abandoning her for a life at sea. She wanted George at home under her watchful eye. Still, Lawrence and the Fairfaxes hoped to enlist George in the navy with Mary Washington's permission. They were aware that she would have many strong objections and that swaying her opinion would be difficult.

George was packed and the commission was made available to him. On September 8, 1746, he left his mother's house at Ferry Farm and boarded a ferry for Fredericksburg. Colonel Fairfax had ridden 25 miles from Belvoir to meet him there. He gave George two letters written by Lawrence Washington. The first letter, addressed to George, contained the reasons Lawrence believed a sea career would be wise for the boy. He hoped the letter would give George the confidence he would need to be forceful when his mother raised objections to his departure. The second letter was to be given to George's mother when he thought she was in an agreeable mood.

George summoned his courage and told his mother about his plans to be a midshipman. As expected, she was not pleased by the idea but was too clever to refuse outright. Instead Mary Washington said she would provide her answer after seeking advice from her older brother in England.

Joseph Ball, a lawyer, answered his sister by saying:

> I understand you are advised and have some thought of sending your son George to sea. I think he had better be put apprentice to a tinker, for a common sailor before the mast has by no means the common liberty of the subject. For they will [impress] him from a ship where he has 50 shillings a month and make him take three and twenty, and [whip] him and staple him and use him . . . like a dog. And as for any considerable preferment in the Navy, it is not to be expected. There are always too many grasping for it here who have interest, and he has none.
>
> And if he should get to be master of a Virginia ship (which will be very difficult to do) a planter that has three or four hundred acres of land and three or four slaves, if he be industrious, may live more comfortably, and leave his family in better bread [than] such a master of a ship can. . . . He must not be hasty to be rich but must go on gently and with patience as things will naturally go. This method, without aiming to be a fine gentleman before his time, will carry a man more comfortably and surely through the world than going to sea.

With her brother's advice in hand, Mary now refused George permission to join the navy. And in the end, the plan to send George off to sea had the unhappy result of driving the family apart. Mary was annoyed with Lawrence and the Fairfaxes for interfering in her life. George was upset with his mother. He left Ferry Farm to move in with Lawrence and Anne. His relationship with his mother remained strained. George would never talk to his Uncle Joseph again.

Belvoir was far fancier than Ferry Farm, where the rooms were small and the occupants didn't wear shoes. Belvoir's residents wore fancy clothes as they traveled the home's

Reenactment of a colonial dance. At Belvoir, the estate of Colonel William Fairfax, the young George Washington was a favorite at such elegant gatherings. Evidently he cut quite a figure: some even claimed he was the finest dancer in the Virginia colony.

drawing rooms, music room, dining room, and well-stocked library. George took full advantage of the opportunity to read the volumes of history he found there. Colonel Fairfax introduced him to Roman history and literature. George read his first play at age 13. It was *Cato: A Tragedy*, and it always had a special place in his heart. The play was about a highly principled general who fought against injustice.

He also borrowed Seneca's *Morals by Way of Abstracts*. Like the *Rules of Civility*, it helped George deal with his anger toward his mother and encouraged him to become more patient.

The colonel issued frequent invitations to George to come over to play the card games of *whist* and *loo*, to go fox hunting, and to spend

> As he grew older, George Washington came to dislike the concept of slavery. He freed his slaves upon his death.

time with the colonel's son, George William Fairfax. Despite an eight-year difference in their ages, they became friends.

When George was 15, Lord Fairfax left his home in England and arrived at Belvoir. He too fell under the spell of the popular young man. Lord Fairfax's passion was fox hunting. He enjoyed the sport so much that before he arrived he sent over three of his favorite English foxhounds. A nobleman's sport, fox hunting is done on horseback, with the hounds using their well-trained noses to find the fox and chase it out of its burrow. Lord Fairfax especially enjoyed George's presence during the hunt because George was an excellent horseman. It was one of the few passions he shared with his mother.

Lord Fairfax also taught George about horse breeding and horse racing. As a man George would pursue these pastimes enthusiastically.

When they got the chance, the Fairfaxes helped George with his career, giving him his first paying job as a surveyor's assistant, and smoothing the way for his appointment as official surveyor of Culpeper County at 17 and his appointment as major in the Virginia *militia* at 20.

To those who said George was too young to be leading men, one of the Fairfaxes reportedly answered, "All Washingtons are born old."

This portrait of
George Washington
by artist Gilbert
Stuart was painted
around 1797, the
year America's first
president retired
from public life.

Reluctant President

Lawrence Washington contracted tuberculosis, a disease of the lungs, and died in 1752. George Washington applied for Lawrence's job in the Virginia militia. He was made a major even though he had no military experience. Eager to acquire some, he soon volunteered to place himself in harm's way in what was to become the French and Indian War.

Like the British, the French also wanted a piece of the New World. They began settling men in the Ohio River valley. To strengthen their position, they made alliances with the Indians. Alarmed, the English asked Virginia's governor, Robert Dinwiddie, to intervene. George volunteered to take a letter to the French from Governor Dinwiddie asking the French to leave the area. Not surprisingly, the French refused Dinwiddie's request.

While delivering the bad news to the governor, George suggested that the English build a fort on the Ohio River to defend their interests in the area. The fort was to be named Fort Necessity. While the fort was being built, Washington led a troop of men there to defend it. On the way there they attacked and killed several French soldiers. But among the dead was a French ambassador, a diplomat who had been trying to deliver a message to the British. Killing an ambassador was a serious violation of the rules of war. A French and Indian force retaliated by attacking Fort Necessity, forcing George to surrender. Disheartened, he resigned from the army.

When England sent General Edward Braddock to the colonies to force the French out, he asked George to be his aide. But he didn't follow George's advice. George knew that the French and Indian armies fought in a looser, less predictable manner than the British. The British were used to fighting in open fields. The French and Indians thought nothing of firing from behind trees. Despite George's warning, Braddock's men were overwhelmed when their enemies attacked. The general died in the battle. George was nearly killed when two horses were shot out from under him. There were four bullet holes in his coat.

The English tried to blame the colonists for the disaster. But the colonists responded by placing George Washington, at 22, in charge of all of Virginia's soldiers.

In 1758, George resigned and returned to Mount Vernon. The French and Indian War continued until 1763, when the British won. The victory gave them control of the land from the eastern coast to the Mississippi River.

George Washington had two horses shot out from under him during the French and Indian War. Blessed with a first-rate immune system, he also survived malaria, smallpox, mumps, and typhoid fever.

Meanwhile, in 1759, George married Martha

General Edward Braddock lost more than half his men, and was himself mortally wounded, in a 1755 engagement with the French and their Indian allies along the Monongahela River. George Washington, an aide to the British general, escaped with his life but found himself unfairly blamed for the disaster.

Custis, a young widow with two children. He became a Virginia legislator and focused his energies on tobacco farming. George, like other colonials, began to see that the British had stacked the rules of commerce against the colonists.

To make up for the cost of the French and Indian War, the British levied new taxes in the American colonies on tea and other necessities. They sent additional troops over from England to keep the colonists from rebelling against the new restrictions.

In 1774, George Washington was one of seven Virginia delegates to the First Continental Congress, which aimed to resolve the colonists' differences with the British. Before the Second Continental Congress could convene a year later, the opening battles of the American Revolution had taken place at Lexington and Concord in Massachusetts. At the second meeting of the Continental Congress, George was chosen to command the Continental forces against the British. He reluctantly accepted, setting the stage for him to lead a ragged, ill-funded army against one of the best-trained fighting forces in the world: the Royal Army of England.

George was a popular general who knew how to keep men fighting when their natural inclination was to desert. Badly beaten by Sir William Howe in New York in August 1776, he was forced to retreat southward through New Jersey and across the Delaware River into Pennsylvania.

By December, the war seemed lost. But on Christmas night, George led his troops back across the Delaware. After a long night march, the Continentals surprised the Hessians— German *mercenaries* fighting for the British—at Trenton, New

Washington Crossing the Delaware, painted by Emanuel Leutze 75 years after the famous events of Christmas 1776, presents an idealized depiction of George Washington and his men on the eve of their victory against the Hessians at Trenton.

Jersey. George's stunning victory at the Battle of Trenton, along with another victory a few days later at Princeton, inspired American patriots to continue the fight.

But many difficult times lay ahead for George Washington and his men. After the British won a battle at Brandywine Creek in Pennsylvania in September 1777, the Continentals were forced to give up Philadelphia. George and his men hunkered down at Valley Forge during the bitter winter of 1777–78. The colonies' fortunes picked up when France joined the war as their allies in 1778. Still, the fighting dragged on for three more years.

Washington, with two of his wife's grandchildren (whom he adopted), inspects the work of his slaves at Mount Vernon. After the Revolutionary War, he intended to settle back into the life of a Virginia planter—but the call of his country once again thrust him into the spotlight.

In the final battle of the Revolutionary War, George surprised a large British force commanded by Lord Cornwallis at Yorktown, Virginia, by quickly moving the Continental army south from New York. Encircled by Washington's foot soldiers on land, and with his escape route at sea cut off by French warships, Cornwallis had few options. On October 19, 1781, as his band played a song called "The World Turned Upside Down," the British general surrendered.

With the war over, George settled back into his old life as planter and husband. He loved farming, which he described as "the most healthy, the most useful, and the most noble employment of men." He liked to find new and better ways to do things on his farm. He developed a two-story, 16-sided barn that allowed horses to thresh wheat, oats, and rye—time-consuming work that normally had to be done by men. He also was among the first people to realize the importance of making fertilizer through composting. George had his slaves gather all the trash at Mount Vernon in one spot, where it could naturally break down into compost.

Once again, though, his retirement was short-lived. After winning independence from Great Britain, the United States had adopted the Articles of Confederation. This document left most governmental power in the hands of the individual states. The federal government was quite weak. The arrangement proved unworkable. For example, when Shays's Rebellion—an uprising among Massachusetts farmers who were deeply in debt—erupted in 1786, the federal government was powerless under the Articles of Confederation to help Massachusetts stop the violence.

By the following year, many American leaders recognized the need for a stronger federal government. Delegates from the states convened in Philadelphia on May 25, 1787, to try to draw up a new federal constitution that would create such a government. George Washington, perhaps the most respected man in all America at this time, was selected to lead the 39 delegates at the Constitutional Convention. After a summer of meetings and debate, the U.S. Constitution was drawn up and signed by the delegates.

The Constitution created a government made up of a legislative branch consisting of the House of Representatives and the Senate, a judicial branch led by the Supreme Court, and an

Washington was the first president to be honored with his face on a U.S. postage stamp. His face also adorns the one-dollar bill.

executive branch headed by the president. But who would be president?

George Washington didn't want the job. This made him an attractive candidate for the electors representing their respective states. They were concerned that an individual who loved power would use the office for his own purposes. George was elected America's first president in 1789 and reelected in 1792. John Adams was his vice president. George picked Alexander Hamilton as his secretary of the Treasury and Thomas Jefferson as his secretary of state.

During his first term, a federal bank was created to issue money and hold federal deposits. Debts assumed by the states to finance the American Revolution were taken over by the federal government.

The nation's capital was moved from New York to Philadelphia until a new capital city could be built in the newly created District of Columbia.

During George's second term, America was asked to come to the aid of its former ally, France, when it declared war on Britain. Instead, George kept the United States neutral, maintaining friendly contact with both warring parties.

His authority as president was tested during the so-called Whiskey Rebellion of 1794, which took place in western Pennsylvania. To help pay the national debt, Congress had ordered a tax on whiskey. The tax was unpopular with farmers who were accustomed to making extra money by distilling

First in the hearts of his countrymen: George Washington's importance in American history remains unsurpassed.

whiskey from corn that would otherwise have spoiled. When attempts were made to collect the tax in Pennsylvania, farmers refused to pay and the governor refused to make them. George sent an army to quell the rebellion and let the people know the federal government meant business.

George Washington delivered a farewell address to the American people on September 17, 1796. With the inauguration of John Adams as president the following March, George retired from public life. He died at Mount Vernon three years later, on December 14, 1799.

He was, as one of his cavalry officers, Harry Lee, described him in his *eulogy*, "First in war, first in peace and first in the hearts of his countrymen."

CHRONOLOGY

1732   George Washington born in Westmoreland County, Virginia, on February 22.

1743   Father dies.

1746   Obtains a commission in the Royal Navy through the influence of his half-brother Lawrence and the wealthy Fairfax family, but his mother refuses to let him go to sea.

1748   Works as surveyor's assistant on expedition to measure the landholdings of Thomas Fairfax west of the Blue Ridge Mountains.

1749   Becomes official surveyor of Culpeper County, Virginia.

1753   Appointed major in the Virginia militia.

1755   Serves as aide to the British general Edward Braddock in a disastrous expedition to force the French from the Ohio River valley.

1759   Marries Martha Custis; becomes a member of the Virginia House of Burgesses.

1774   Becomes a member of Continental Congress.

1775 –81   As commander of the Continental army, leads his troops to eventual victory over the British in the Revolutionary War; accepts the surrender of Lord Cornwallis at Yorktown, Virginia, in October 1781.

1787   President of Constitutional Convention.

1789   Elected the first president of the United States and takes office on April 30.

1792   Reelected to second term as president.

1796   Gives farewell address.

1799   Dies at Mount Vernon, Virginia, on December 14.

GLOSSARY

burgess—a representative in the colonial Virginia legislature.

coroner—an officer of the crown who investigated suspicious deaths.

eulogy—a speech given about someone who has recently died.

geometry—a branch of mathematics that deals with the measurement and properties of points, lines, angles, surfaces, and solids.

Jesuit—a member of a Roman Catholic men's religious order founded in 1534 and charged with teaching and missionary work.

legislator—a member of a law-making body in the local, state, or national government.

loo—a card game, played with three to eight people, that was popular during the 17th to 19th centuries.

mare—an adult female horse.

mercenaries—soldiers who fight for a country other than their own purely for money.

militia—a nonprofessional army composed of local citizens.

plantation—a large southern farm run with the help of slaves.

sanctuary—a safe place or refuge.

surveyor—a person who measures land for development.

trigonometry—a branch of mathematics that deals with the properties of triangles, arcs, and angles.

tuberculosis—a disease of the lungs that is transmitted from one person to another.

vestryman—a church leader who is not a member of the clergy.

whist—a four-player card game played with two teams.

FURTHER READING

Brookheiser, Richard. *Founding Father: Rediscovering George Washington.*
New York: The Free Press, 1996.

Clark, Harrison. *All Cloudless Glory: The Life of George Washington from Youth to Yorktown.* Washington, D.C.: Regnery Publishing, 1995.

Hannaford, Peter. *The Essential George Washington.* Bennington, Vt.: Images from the Past Inc., 1999.

Hilton, Suzanne. *The World of Young George Washington.* New York: Walker & Co., 1987.

Marcovitz, Hal. *The Constitution.* Philadelphia: Mason Crest Publishers, 2003.

Randall, Willard Sterne. *George Washington: A Life.* New York: Henry Holt & Co., 1997.

Rubel, David. *Scholastic Encyclopedia of the Presidents and Their Times.* New York: Agincourt Press, 1994.

Schlesinger, Arthur M., jr., et al, editors. *The Elections of 1789 & 1792.* Philadelphia: Mason Crest Publishers, 2003.

- http://www.fieldtrip.com/pa/54934076.htm
  Washington Crossing Park

- http://www.firstladies.org/MARTHA_WASHINGTON/FL.HTML
  First lady Martha Washington

- http://www.house.gov/petri/gw_home.htm
  Essays on the life of George Washington

- http://www.americanpresident.org/kotrain/courses/GW/GW_In_Brief.htm
  Biography of George Washington from the television show *The American President*

- http://www.mountvernon.org
  Mount Vernon

- http://earlyamerica.com/lives/gwlife/index.html
  An account of the life of George Washington written by one of his contemporaries

- http://www.surfnetkids.com/washing.htm
  Washington website for fifth graders

- http://www.whitehouse.gov/history/presidents/gw1.html
  The White House Biography of George Washington

INDEX

Adams, John, 23, 40, 41
American Revolution, 23, 36–38, 40
Articles of Confederation, 39

Ball, Joseph (uncle), 29
Ball, William (great-grandfather), 15
Belvoir, 26, 27, 28, 29–30, 31
Blue Ridge Mountains, 9, 10
Braddock, Edward, 34
Brandywine Creek, battle of, 37

Cato: A Tragedy, 30
Charles I, king of England, 15, 27
Charles II, king of England, 27
Constitutional Convention, 23, 39
Cornwallis, Lord Charles, 38
Culpeper County, Virginia, 13, 31

Dinwiddie, Robert, 33

England, 15, 21, 23, 25, 36
English civil war, 15, 27
Epsewasson, 18, 25. *See also* Mount
    Vernon
Eskridge, George, 17

Fairfax, George William, 31
Fairfax, Lord Thomas, 9, 13, 26, 31
Fairfax, Colonel William, 26, 28, 30,
    31
Ferry Farm, 25, 27, 28, 29
First Continental Congress, 36
Fort Necessity, 33, 34
French and Indian War, 33–34, 36

Genn, James, 9

Hamilton, Alexander, 40
Howe, Sir William, 36

Jackson, Andrew, 23

Jefferson, Thomas, 19, 23, 40

Lee, Harry, 41

Morals by Way of Abstracts (Seneca),
    30
Mount Vernon, 18, 25, 26, 34, 39, 41

Native Americans, 13, 33–34, 36
New Jersey, 9, 36–37

Parliament, 15
Pennsylvania, 36
Princeton, battle of, 37
Puritan Revolution, 15. *See also*
    English civil war

*Rules of Civility and Decent Behavior in
    Company and Conversation*,
    22–23, 30

Second Continental Congress, 36
Scotland, 15
Seahorse of London, 15
Shays's Rebellion, 39
Shenandoah Valley, 9

Trenton, battle of, 36–37

U.S. Constitution, 39–40

Valley Forge, 37
Virginia, 9, 13, 15, 16, 25, 29, 31, 34,
    36

Washington, Anne Fairfax, 26, 29
Washington, Augustine "Gus"
    (father), 16, 21, 25, 26, 27, 28,
    29, 33
Washington, Augustine Jr. (half
    brother), 16, 21

Washington, Betty (sister), 17
Washington, Charles (brother), 17
Washington, George
  birth of, 15, 16–17
  childhood legends about, 17, 19
  education of, 21, 22–23
  military career of, 23, 31, 33–34,
    36–38
  and plan to join the British navy,
    27–29
  and plantation life, 18, 19, 29–31
  political career of, 36, 39–41
  as president, 13, 23, 39–41
  as surveyor, 9–10, 11–13, 31
Washington, Jack (brother), 17
Washington, Jane (half sister), 16, 18
Washington, John (great-grandfather),
    15–16

Washington, Lawrence (grandfather),
    16
Washington, Lawrence (half brother),
    16, 21, 25, 26, 27, 28, 29, 33
Washington, Martha Custis (wife), 36
Washington, Mary Ball (mother), 16,
    17, 19, 21, 28
Washington, Mildred (sister), 17–18
Washington, Samuel (brother), 17
Weems, Mason, 19
Whiskey Rebellion, 40–41
William and Mary College, 13
Williamsburg, 13

Yorktown, battle of, 38

Contributors

ARTHUR M. SCHLESINGER JR. holds the Albert Schweitzer Chair in the Humanities at the Graduate Center of the City University of New York. He is the author of more than a dozen books, including *The Age of Jackson*; *The Vital Center*; *The Age of Roosevelt* (3 vols.); *A Thousand Days: John F. Kennedy in the White House*; *Robert Kennedy and His Times*; *The Cycles of American History*; and *The Imperial Presidency*. Professor Schlesinger served as  Special Assistant to President Kennedy (1961–63). His numerous awards include the Pulitzer Prize for History; the Pulitzer Prize for Biography; two National Book Awards; the Bancroft Prize; and the American Academy of Arts and Letters Gold Medal for History.

GAIL SNYDER is a freelance writer and advertising copywriter. This is her first book. She lives in Chalfont, Pennsylvania, with her husband, Hal, and children Michelle and Ashley.